3 Day Guide to Budapest

A 72-hour definitive guide on what to see, eat and enjoy in Budapest, Hungary

3 DAY CITY GUIDES

Copyright © 2014 BeautyBodyStyle, LLC

All rights reserved. No part of this book may be reproduced in any form or by any electronic or mechanical means including information storage and retrieval systems – except in the case of brief quotations in articles or reviews – without the permission in writing from its publisher.

Although the author and publisher have made every effort to ensure that the information in this book was correct at press time, the author and publisher do not assume and hereby disclaim any liability to any party for any loss, damage, or disruption caused by errors or omissions, whether such errors or omissions result from negligence, accident, or any other cause.

Cover Photo Credits:

Dennis Jarvis St. Stephen's Basilica Dome. Image use under CC-BY License via Flickrr

Panoramas Smiling Child Statue. Image use under CC-BY License via Flickrr

Moyan Brenn Budapest Sunset. Image use under CC BY-ND License via Flickrr

Moyan Brenn Budapest Vaci Utca. Image use under CC BY-ND License via Flickrr

ISBN: 1503316629
ISBN-13: 978-1503316621

"A journey of a thousand miles starts with a single step." – Lao Tzu

CONTENTS

1	Budapest Introduction	1
2	Delve Into the Medieval Past of Budapest	16
3	The Hidden Treasures and Off the Beaten Paths of Budapest	30
4	The Late Night Surprises of Danube's Queen	41
5	Artsy Relaxation & A Lavish Shopping Spree	47
6	The Best Places to Dine in Hungary's Food Capital	56
7	Where to Enjoy a Good Night's Sleep in Budapest	63
8	Conclusion	69
9	More from This Author	71

1 BUDAPEST INTRODUCTION

Fisherman's Bastion and Chain Bridge. Photo credit: Dennis Jarvis via Flickrr

Budapest, the capital of Hungary, is a blissful hub drenched in natural beauty, culture and history. Famous for its animated and youthful vibe, this Hungarian epicenter also has a nightlife scene that will keep you grooving until the wee hours of the morning. Yet, for its buzz and energy, the city remains a laid-back sanctuary, thanks to its fin-de-siècle aura and sparkling natural hot springs.

Romanticized for its imperial beauty, the city of Budapest has an abundance of historic monuments and architectural masterpieces on display, such as the Parisi udvar and Fisherman's Bastion. A rich lode of man-made beauties, Budapest is specked with art nouveau, eclectic, neoclassical and baroque buildings to please everyone's artistic appetite. Nicknamed as the "Pearl of the Danube", you will find an array of unusual and intriguing building details, from the WWII shrapnel scorings and bullet holes to the neoclassical bas-reliefs and glazed tiles.

Praised as a food capital since the 19th century, this Hungarian haven boasts of enticing local goodies, including gulyas, Balaton pike-perch and paprikas. Besides its mouthwatering Hungarian gastronomic staples, the city has a wide variety of international cuisines as well, from Chinese to French.

Budapest isn't called as the "City of Spas" for nothing. Blessed with a wealth of hot springs, this magnificent city boasts over 400 mineral and 120 thermal springs from 14 various sources. What's more, it is one of the few places on the face of the earth where you can indulge in traditional Turkish baths that date back more than 300 years ago, such as Veli Bejj, Kiraly and Rudas.

While you're here, why not spend an unforgettable night with the nocturnal tourists and night owls of the city at any of its chic and pulsating nightlife venues? If you are looking for an out-of-the-ordinary nightlife experience, dance your way to an unforgettable night cruise along the Danube River.

Looking for a great place to chill out, and drink a few glasses of beer? Then, head off to the Red Ruin bar, and choose from their endless selection of cocktails as well as Hungarian beers and cocktails.

If you want to delve into the gripping history of Hungary, a visit to this city gives you a peek at the events of the Second World War as well as the uprising in 1956. There are a lot of reminders of its bloody past, such as the House of Terror and the Danube memorial's poignant Shoes on the Danube. In contrast, Budapest also has a cluster of historic offerings that epitomize the city's reconciliation and hope, such as the Buda Castle Hill Funicular,

Hungarian State Opera, and Budapest History Museum.

The Shoes on the Danube is a memorial on the bank of the Danube River in Budapest. It honors the Jews who were killed by fascist Arrow Cross militiamen in Budapest during World War II. They were ordered to take off their shoes, and were shot at the edge of the water so that their bodies fell into the river and were carried away. It represents their shoes left behind on the bank. Photo credit: Dennis Jarvis via Flickrr

One of the most popular destinations in Europe, the city of Budapest is indeed a beautiful, vibrant and colorful destination that will bombard you in a myriad of ways. After all, it was listed as a UNESCO World Heritage Site in 1987, for the architectural and cultural significance of the Andrassy Avenue, Buda Castle Quarter, and the Banks of the Danube. Moreover, it has a sophisticated style and a picturesque setting, earning the moniker of "Paris of the East". So, if you are looking for an eclectic destination that can rival Paris and the other top destinations in the world, look no further than Budapest.

History

The history of Budapest isn't boring by any means, even though it was officially declared as a city in 1873, with the integration of Obuda, Pest and Buda. For several centuries, these three parts of the city were developing and reforming separately. As with other cities in Europe, this Hungarian apple experienced a great deal of liberations, invasions and barbarous wars. And, yet, she always finds a way to survive and revive in a rather compelling fashion. As a result of this eternal cycle of demolitions and rebirths, Budapest has formed a mesmerizing cityscape that millions of tourists have now adored. Today, you can still see traces of the city's fascinating and colorful history, from its cobbled streets to grandiose buildings.

What are the city's origins? With its strategic and favorable location, Budapest has always been a prized area of human settlement. As a matter of fact, this area has been inhabited by a heap of human civilizations since 500,000 BC, including Celts and Illyrians. The written history of this region, however, only started during the Roman invasion in 35 BC. While the ancient Romans only stayed in Budapest for two centuries, you can still see some of the traces they have left, and feel their influence in the city.

The Roman regime, eventually, collapsed in the 4th century, allowing Huns and other tribes to settle in the territory. In 9th century, the Magyars, the ancestors of today's Hungarians, settled in the Carpathian Basin along the Danube River. Spearheaded by St. Stephen (Hungary's first king), the Magyars established a strong state in this region.

Everything was going well for the Magyars in the earlier stages of the Middle Ages, until the Mongols attacked and devastated the entire country. Not only did they conquer the Transdanubian area, but they destroyed Pest and Buda as well. The Mongols decimated the Magyar population, and burnt their crops, causing famine following the raids. Fortunately, their Khan died unexpectedly, and they returned to Asia. Later on, King Bela IV restored the country, and built a strong fortress on the hills of Buda, bolstering their defense against future raids.

Budapest flourished under the rule of King Matthias in the 15th century. Buda became the epicenter of arts, culture and politics of contemporary Europe. Pest, on the other hand, was viewed as commercial center of the country.

But once again, the city was in hot waters, when an enemy came into view at Hungary's borders. In 1526, the Turks ravaged Hungary, and defeated its vast army. The Turks settled in Budapest for over a hundred years, and introduced a handful of exotic traditions to the Hungarians.

Trail-blazed by the Roman Emperor, a Christian army liberated Pest and Buda in 1686. Unfortunately, these two towns were destroyed in this siege. Even Castle Hill's glittering Royal Palace was left in ruins following the so-called rescue. To make matters worse, the siege didn't bring freedom to the country, as it was anointed as one of the provinces of the Habsburg Empire. The city finally became independent in 1867.

In 1873, the cities, Obuda, Buda and pest were united, becoming the capital city of Hungary. From 1873 to 1914, the city enjoyed its golden age, flourishing like never before. In this era, splendid architectures were sprouting everywhere, new roads and boulevards were made, and the first Metro in Europe was built.

The city somehow survived and restored its grandeur, amidst the two World Wars and the 1956 uprising. What is even more surprising is the fact that it was able to retain its reputation as a gastronomic destination. In the 1990s, it was highly viewed as one of the premier tourist destinations in all of Europe.

Climate and seasons

Sheltered by the Alps and isolated by the Carpathian Basin, Budapest has a temperate climate that would favor sightseers and adventurists. But, its weather is also a bit capricious, with Mediterranean, continental and oceanic climatic zones affecting it. Still, there haven't been a lot of complaints pertaining to the climate of Budapest.

Budapest, like the rest of Hungary, has four seasons, namely winter, autumn, summer, and spring. The climate is normally hot during summer, and cool or warm in autumn and spring, with an average temperature of 11 degrees Celsius (52 degrees Fahrenheit). For an Eastern European city, the city is quite sunny, with over 2,000 hours of sun per year.

Wondering when is the best time to visit Budapest? Unlike most locations in the continent, this Hungarian metropolis is a year-round destination, with a relatively moderate climate, and a plethora of events happening throughout the four seasons. Locals, though, think it is best to visit it in early autumn and spring.

Budapest rises and shines from its deep winter slumber during the spring season, which starts from March and ends in May. With day temperatures ranging from 20 to 25 degrees Celsius

(68 to 77 degrees Fahrenheit), tourists can enjoy warm and sunny days during this season. Plus, the city will have grass, trees, and spring flowers all in shades of green, providing a refreshing break after the grey days of winter. However, the climate in March and in the first two weeks of April is a little unpredictable.

Spring and autumn might be the most recommended times to visit the city, but most international travelers come to Budapest during summertime (June-August). Of course, summer in this city is dry and hot, with daily temperature that may go beyond 30 degrees Celsius (86 degrees Fahrenheit).

As a destination, Budapest is extremely appealing during autumn, which is from September to November. With the summer crowds heading home, visitors can easily find great deals on accommodations in this season. Also, it still has warm weather, with a day average of 24 degrees Celsius (75 degrees Fahrenheit).

With an average temperature that ranges from negative 10 to degrees Celsius (14 to 41 degrees

Fahrenheit), it's safe to say that winter is the least popular time to visit this boom town. Apparently, the city's winter is very chilly, snowy, rainy and windy. But, wintertime offers the cheapest rates for rooms, restaurants and attractions. Not to mention, winter is a great opportunity to snap a few scenic photographs.

Language

Visiting Budapest soon? Make sure to invest in an English-to-Hungarian dictionary. Also, don't worry much about your inability to speak Hungarian, as most of its locals can understand English.

Getting In

How can you reach Budapest? Well, there are a number of ways to reach this city, from airplanes to boats. The fastest and most convenient way to travel to this capital is to take a plane ride bound for Budapest Franz Liszt International Airport (BUD), the largest airport in the country. As an international airport, it connects Budapest to several international cities in Middle East, Africa, America and Europe. Likewise, it is a host to several commercial airlines, including Air France,

Japan Airlines, American Airlines, and more. For more information about the airport's schedule and airlines, visit their website: http://www.bud.hu/.

Scared of flying? Hop on a train destined for the Budapest Keleti station. At this station, there are trains that connect the city to cities in eastern and central Europe, including Munich, Berlin, Vienna, Warsaw, Belgrade and more. Additionally, the city has a trio of railway stations that link it to many countries in the continent, namely the Nyugati Palyaudvar, Deli Palyaudvar, and Keleti Palyaudvar. For prices and list of cities that are connected to these stations, visit: http://www.raileurope-asean.com/city/budapest?lang=en&var_mode=calcul and http://www.elvira.hu/.

Operating under the management of Volan Station, Hungary has a national bus network that transports travelers to Budapest from other cities of the country. Furthermore, there are a few bus companies that have routes to international cities. Eurolines has daily trips from and to Slovakia and Austria. Orangeways, meanwhile, connects the city to Slovakia, Poland, Netherlands, Germany,

Croatia, Czech Republic and Austria.

Contact number/ website:

    Eurolines: +36 1 318 2122

    Orangeways: +36 30 830 9696

    Volan Association: http://www.volan.eu/

You can reach Budapest by taking a hydrofoil service from Bratislava or Vienna to the Danube River. This boat trip, however, is scheduled and only available between April and November. Interested in testing out your sea legs? Call Mahart with this number: +36 1 484 4000.

Getting around

Are you a nomadic soul who loves to travel on foot? Walking along Budapest's streets is by far the best and most effective way to get a load of the city's population and electrifying life. In fact, the city's amusing pedestrian traffic may harvest its own lovely photographs. Besides, most of the city's top sites and attractions are within walking distance to each other, helping you reduce your transportation costs. As you make your way around the city on foot, just be sure to bring a paper map of the destination or a phone with a GPS.

Not overly fond of walking? Thankfully, BKV Zrt, the city's public transportation system, offers cheap metro, tram and bus services all over the city. Before you hop on a public transportation service, though, make sure to have your tickets validated. Inspectors may suddenly show up, and impose hefty fines for tickets that are not validated. Also, purchase your tickets ahead of time at a newsstand or metro station, as they might not be available onboard. As for the price, a one-way ticket usually costs around 260 to 400 HUF. Check their website: http://bkv.hu/en/prices/2013_en, to get listing of their prices and routes.

Do you want to drive around and explore the city at your own will? Renting a car may seem a viable option to get around the city but it's not as practical, and can be a bit inconvenient, with the city's heavy traffic, especially in the late afternoons and mornings. Also, you need to have a solid know-how about their driving rules and etiquette.

Taxis are a dime a dozen in the city of Budapest. As

a tourist, these cabs certainly can come in handy during your trip. However be sure to hire only a legitimate and regulated taxi, as there are many unauthorized taxi drivers that would overcharge naïve travelers. The registered and genuine cabs are those with yellow taxi signs and license plates, as well as ID badges on their dashboards.

With Budapest's burgeoning network of cycling paths, it is no wonder more and more of the city's dwellers are using bicycles as their primary means of transportation. The city's main roads are a bit unnerving and busy for inexperienced cyclists, but there are a few areas where biking may be pleasurable, such as Margaret Island and City Park.

2 DELVE INTO THE MEDIEVAL PAST OF BUDAPEST

Is it possible to experience Budapest in three days? Travelers, who only arrange a two-day itinerary in Hungary's capital, usually leave unhappily, and would vow to stay longer for their future visit. With dozens of mesmerizing sights and fascinating attractions laid out all over the city, a three-day trip to Budapest may seem like an unfruitful and downbeat foray.

However with the right travel plan, you will be able to maximize your trip, and observe the city from a local's perspective. What's more, you will able to get a full taste of all the celebrated landmarks and attractions of the city.

For the first day of trip to the Budapest, you will be delving into the intriguing medieval history of the city with stops to monumental historic sites like the Castle Hill, Fisherman's Bastion, Matthias Church and Royal Palace. To get heavier dose of the history of Hungary and its capital, you'll be dropping by the Budapest History Museum and National Gallery. Then, you are going to cap off your day with a sojourn and short walk along the most beloved and significant sight of the city.

Eat your breakfast

Before you embark on an unforgettable journey to this destination, first you need to get some nourishment by eating breakfast at your hotel or hostel. Don't like the breakfast served at your rented enclave? Muvesz Kavehaz Restaurant, one of the oldest cafes in the city, serves delightful cakes, coffee and breakfast. Moreover, the café has a fantastic ambiance with elegant decorations.

Additional information about Muvesz

Address: Andrassy ut 29, Budapest, Hungary

Contact number: +36 1 343 544

Opening hours: 9 am to 10 pm from Monday to Saturday. 10 am to 10 pm on Sunday.

Recommended time of arrival: 9 am

Duration: 20 to 30 minutes

Make your way to the Castle Hill

Want to start your trip on a positive note? Then, make your way to the world-famous Castle Hill on the Buda side of the city. A UNESCO World Heritage Site, the Castle Hill is truly a symbol of city's gripping medieval past. Characterized by classical and baroque buildings, lovely squares, narrow alleys and cobblestone streets, this red-letter site is packed with interesting museums as well as historic attractions and sights. As a bonus, you will be treated with great panoramas of the river and city.

How to get there:

Since cars are not allowed to enter the area, you have to travel to Castle Hill either by walking, taking a taxi or hopping on public transport. If you are traveling from Pest, the most convenient way to get to this district is to board bus 16 from Deak Ferenc ter, and disembark at Disz ter's terminal stop. Another way to reach this district is to jump on metro M2, get off Moszkva ter, and take a walk along I Varfok utca to the admirable Vienna Gate.

Looking for a fun way to get to Castle Hill? Stroll leisurely across the striking Chain Bridge, and take the Siklo, a 19th century cable railway that lifts off from Clark Adam ter and takes you to Szent Gyorgy ter. As an alternative, you may take a hike up to the Kiraly lepcso (the Royal Steps), or the wide stairway that leads to the Royal Palace's southern end from I Szarvas ter.

A deluge of medieval exhibits and jewels

Fortifications at Buda Castle. Photo credit: <u>Ben</u> via Flickrr

The Royal Castle, or also referred as Buda Castle, is definitely an edifice you cannot afford to miss in Budapest. Famous for its long history and impressive architecture, this iconic site offers an array of attractions to its visitors, such as the Turul Bird's statue, a King Matthias bronze statue, Matthias Well, and the Lion Courtyard. More importantly, it is home to a trio of treasuries, the National Library, Budapest History Museum, and Hungarian National Gallery.

Located in Building E of the castle, the Budapest History Museum may not be one of the top-rated museums in the city. Nonetheless, it is a treasury worth swinging by. Here, you get to lay eyes on a decent collection of restored medieval rooms.

To get an in-depth scoop of the Hungary's art history, make your way to the Palace's National Gallery. Designed to feature the development and history of Hungarian painting, this gallery houses a collection that illustrates the past five centuries of art in the country, including Gothic altars, Gothic wooden sculptures, as well as Renaissance and Medieval stonework. A word of advice when visiting this gallery, keep an eye out for the exquisite carnival paintings of Vilmos Aba-Novak, overly wrought heroic paintings from Gyula Benczur, and Tivadar Csontvary's religious canvases.

Additional information:

Address: Szent Gyorgy ter 6, Budapest 1014, Hungary

Webpage: http://www.muemlekem.hu/muemlek?id=138

Recommended time of arrival: 10 to 10:15 am

Duration: 1 to 2 hours

Opening hours: The courtyards are open for 24 hours a day, and seven days a week. But, the palace's treasure troves have a corresponding schedule.

National Gallery: 10 am to 6 pm from Tuesday to Sunday.

History Museum: 10 am to 6 pm Tuesday to Sunday (March to October), 10 am to 4 pm Tuesday to Sunday (November of February)

Admission: Except for the galleries and museums, admissions to all the Palace's attractions are free.

Budapest History Museum admission: 2,000

HUF

National Gallery: Permanent exhibits cost 1,000 HUF. Temporary exhibits cost 2,000 HUF

Eat your lunch at a district canteen

Stomach grumbling? Feast on a hearty, appetizing and affordable meal in the heart of Castle Hill at a district canteen near the Mathias Church. For less than 1,000 HUF, you can enjoy a delicious Hungarian main course with a hot soup.

The canteen is located above the Fortuna passage. From the Hess Adras ter, head off to the first yard at the street (there is yellow building with a Fortuna label on it). Before you enter the yard, climb up on the stairs on your left side. There, you will find the canteen, which showcases a bright and spacious room.

Additional information:

Address: Castle District canteen, Fortuna utca 4, Budapest

Map:http://www.spottedbylocals.com/budapest/map/spot/castle-district-canteen

Opening hours: 11:30 am to 2:30 pm from Monday to Friday

Recommended time of arrival: 1 pm

Duration: 20 minutes to 1 hour

If your first day falls on a weekend, look for other restaurants in the area. As one of the trendy tourist spots in the city, Castle Hill offers a variety of restaurants to its visitors.

A church that symbolizes Budapest's rich past

Matthias Church. Photo credit: alcuin lai via Flickrr

After indulging in a gratifying meal at a district canteen, it's time for you to move on with your journey and explore the other medieval treasures of the city. For your next stop, you will be paying homage to one of the oldest buildings in the district, the Matthias Church. Built in 14th century, this 700-year old church has witnessed plenty of royal events, such as the coronations of the kings of Hungary, and King Matthias Corvinus' two weddings.

Dominating the Castle area's main square, this antique building is famed for its graceful and slender gothic architecture. One of the visual highlights of the city, this building also has an interior that is as breathtaking as its architecture. Once you're inside, you can admire the gleaming Hungarian crown jewels, lavishly frescoed ceilings and walls, as well as intricately made murals. What's more, the church has a museum that showcases works from the country's most notable painters.

Additional information:

Address: Szentharomsag ter 2, Budapest 1014,

Hungary

Contact number: +36 1 355 5657

Opening hours: 9 am to 5 pm Monday to Friday. 9 am to 1 pm Saturday. 1 to 5 pm Sunday.

Admission fees: 1,000 HUF for adults, free for children (6 years old and below), 700 HUF for students and seniors

Recommended time of arrival: 2 to 2:30 pm

Duration: 1 hour

Before you go to this historic church, take time to enjoy a casual stroll alongside the awe-inspiring winding streets near it.

Fisherman's Bastion. Photo credit: <u>alcuin lai</u> via Flickrr

Lauded as one of the most celebrated landmarks in Budapest, the Fisherman's Bastion is a splendid lookout and masquerade that draws hordes of tourists every day. While the landmark is only a hundred years old, most viewers think it's much older, due to its rustic design and style. Blending perfectly with the cobbled streets and buildings in Castle Hill, this 19th century building has a touch of medieval to it, thanks to its neo-Gothic design.

What can you do in this romantic castle? Reminiscent of the Disney World's fairytale castles, the bastion is an absolute sightseer's delight, with its classy turrets and pointer towers. Furthermore, it is terrific vantage point where voyagers can appreciate dramatic overlooking views of the Danube River and the entire city.

Additional information:

Tarnork Utca 28, Budapest, Hungary

Opening hours: Open day and night, all year round

Website: http://www.fishermansbastion.com/

Admissions: The 7 140-meter towers and most of its balconies are available to the public for free. The turrets and upper towers, however, have a small and affordable entrance fee of 700 HUF

From Matthias church, you can reach the bastion with a short one-minute walk.

Recommended time of arrival: 3 to 3:30 pm

Duration: 1 to 2 hours

The most recognizable feat of engineering in Hungary

Chain Bridge. Photo credit: <u>Klearchos Kapoutsis</u> via Flickrr

No trip to the city of Budapest is complete without crossing the astonishing Chain Bridge. A world-famous engineering feat, this noteworthy suspension bridge not only has interesting details, but also provides romantic views. Connecting Buda to Pest, this bride is without a doubt the most recognizable sight in the city of Budapest.

Additional information:

> Address: Over the Danube River, between Roosevelt ter and Clark Adam ter, Budapest, Hungary

Recommended time of arrival: 6 to 7 pm. The best time to visit the suspension bride is in the evening, when it lights beautifully illuminate the bridge.

Duration: 1 hour

The Chain Bridge is within walking distance from the Fisherman's Bastion. A 10-minute walk, the distance from the bastion to the bridge is only 800 meters. But, if you are not in the mood for walking, take the next public transport from Szentharomsag ter to Clark Adam ter.

3 THE HIDDEN TREASURES AND OFF THE BEATEN PATHS OF BUDAPEST

Typical international out-of-towners come to Budapest only to behold and explore the city's rhapsodized historic attractions, such as the Fisherman's Bastion and Chain Bridge. Little do they know, Hungary's crown jewel also has a wonderful array of off the beaten paths that are often unseen by international tourists. While these hidden jewels don't get a lot of attention from travel guides and blogs, they are nevertheless just as appealing and interesting as their vintage and hyped counterparts. For your second- day adventure to this capital, you will have an up close encounter with some of the best underrated sensations of Budapest.

Szabadsag Square. Photo credit: Top Budapest via Flickrr

Wake up, smell the coffee, eat your breakfast, and make your way to Bank Center at the Szabadsag Square. One of the most spectacular contemporary landmarks of the country, the Bank Center is an eye-catching mixture of granite, marble, steel and glass, focused all over a dazzling atrium. Designed by the highly acclaimed architect Dr. Jozsef Finta, this modern stunner is a worthy match to the neighboring gorgeous buildings like the former Stock Exchange Palace and National Bank of Hungary.

Additional information

Address: 1054 Szabadsag ter 7, Budapest, Hungary

Contact number: +36 1 302 9010

Recommended time of arrival: 8 to 8:30 am

Duration: 15 to 20 minutes

The building can be accessed easily by public transportation systems, such as tramway 2A and 2, metro line blue 2, bus, as well as trolley buses (78, 73, 72 and 70)

Wander around the square

After taking selfies and photographs of this modern beauty, wander around the Szabadsag Square. Not only is the square a home to a lush park, but is also ringed by a few significant and beautiful buildings, such as the US Embassy and the former Stock Exchange building. Plus, it has a few art nouveau buildings and a couple of shapely monuments dedicated for Harry Hill Bandholtz and Ronald Reagan.

Duration: 30 to 40 minutes

Take photographs of a shiny steel superstructure

ING headquarters in Budapest. Photo credit: <u>Misibacsi</u>

The ING headquarters is arguably the city's finest and most famous modern architectural masterpiece. Built in 2004, this modern treasure it not only loved by its local dwellers, but has met with global recognition as well. A headquarter of a renowned Dutch insurance company, ING headquarters is popular for its awe-inspiring exterior aesthetic appearance, featuring a three-part façade clenched together with heaps of lines of stainless steel. To make it more interesting, it comes with a resplendent and distorted pattern.

Additional information:

Address: Dozsa Gyorgy ut 84c, 1068, Budapest, Hungary

Recommended time of arrival: 9:40 to 10:20 am

Duration: 10 to 20 minutes

From Szabadsag ter, you can reach this spot either by walking, renting a cab, or taking a bus

A visit to the oldest museum in Hungary

Technically, the Hungarian National Museum isn't one of the modern attractions in the city of Budapest. Opened in 1847, this museum is the oldest public museum in the country. But since you are just a few meters away from this museum, you might want to drop by here, and spend an hour marveling at its permanent exhibits, including the Coronation Mantle, ceramics, metalwork, weapons, textiles and furniture. Besides, its building boasts a striking neo-classic architectural design that will leave you in awe.

Additional information:

Address: Muzeum korut 14-16, Budapest IX, Hungary

Contact number: +36 1 338 2122

Opening hours: 10 am to 6 pm from Tuesday to Sunday

Recommended time of arrival: 11 am

Duration: 1 hour

Admission fee: 1,100 HUF, 550 HUF for seniors and students, free for children 6 years old and below.

Eat your lunch

Need to take a lunch break? There are plenty of restaurants that are located near the museum, such as Ruben, Borsso Bistro and Museum Café & Restaurant.

Recommended time of arrival: 12:20 pm

Duration: 30 minutes to 1 hour

Walk the tracks of a reformed palace

neighborhood

Paul street boys sculpture, Budapest, 8. district, Práter street school. Photo credit: Misibacsi

A decade ago, tourists were highly advised to stay away from the streets of Budapest's 8 district, or also called as Jozsefvaros. Underneath the shadows of the district's ornate residences and grandiose aristocratic homes walked homeless people, drug users and prostitutes. But over the past three years, the district has drastically changed its defiled scenery, with art spaces and breezy cafés wadding a neighborhood loaded down with faded charm. Though this neighborhood isn't as popular as Gellert Hill and Castle Hill, it's a burgeoning tourist zone overflowing with eyeful sights.

What to do in this up-and-coming tourist neighborhood? For starters, you can take a leisurely walk along its streets, and gaze on the grand mansions and palaces built during the Austro-Hungarian Empire, such as the Hotel Palazzo Zichy, Italian Cultural Institute, Karolyi Palace and Hungarian Radio. Likewise, you can drop by the Mikszath Square, enjoy a cup of coffee at any of its stylish cafes, and observe the city culture of Budapest.

Additional information:

Jozsefvaros, Budapest, Hungary

Opening hours: Open 24/7

Recommended time of arrival: 2 pm

Duration: 2 hours

From the museum, you can get to this district by taking a bus (909, 83 or 9). Also, you can take a 2-kilomter walk if you prefer to see rare sights of the city.

A stopover at the ultimate Hungarian cultural epicenter

The Palace of Arts, Budapest, Hungary. Photo credit: Vadaro

The Palace of Arts is, hands down, the ultimate cultural hub in Budapest. Housed in a grandiose contemporary architecture, the palace is brimming with eclectic and fascinating exhibits from its institutions that include the Festival Theatre, Ludwig Museums and Beal Bartok National Concert Hall. Likewise, it is a host to one of Europe's most distinguished concert organs. On top of it all, it features a variety of cultural events, including dance, jazz, music, classical music and opera performances.

Additional information:

Address: Komor Marcell u.1., Budapest 1095, Hungary

Contact number: +36 1 555 3300

Website: https://www.mupa.hu/

Opening hours: 10 am to 6 pm

Admission fee: Tours are free, but you have to book early by calling their number or sending an email to info@mupa.hu. As for the organ, tours are also free, but you have to make reservations by reaching them through this email, orgonavezetes@mupa.hu.

Recommended time of arrival: 3:30 to 4 pm

Duration: 1:30 to 2 hours

You can get there by taking Boraros ter's Suburban railway bound for the Lagymanyosi Bridge Station. Also, you may take Streetcar 2 to the Millenniumi Kulturalis Kozpont station.

In the wake of your mind-blowing tour in the Palace of Arts, take a siesta, and gear up for an unforgettable night of partying at one of Europe's nightlife capitals.

4 THE LATE NIGHT SURPRISES OF DANUBE'S QUEEN

Szimpla Kert. Photo credit: <u>Emily Allen</u> via Flickrr

When nightfall rolls in, the city of Budapest shifts gears, transforming into a heaven for socialites and night owls. From plush dance clubs to open-air music lounges and ethereal jazz bars, Budapest bombards party goers with a diverse nightlife scene that will suit everyone's taste.

Overview

Drawing a trendy and young crowd, the city's popular 7th district has a buzzing bohemian scene, and is home to a cluster of stylish nightlife venues. A handful of modish spots can also be found in Kiraly, Wesselenyi and Dob utcas. On the Buda part, the River Danube's bank offers electrifying boat clubs and bars with lively and young crowds. Do you love to gamble? The city has a surfeit of casinos housed in luxury hotels between the Elizabeth Bridge and Chain Bridge, and along Dunakorzo.

Where to enjoy a night out in Budapest? Check out these suggestions.

An innovative nightlife mainstay

Szimpla Kert is the undisputed star of the city's glamorous nightlife scene. Admired for its eccentric style, this nightlife venue is a revolutionary rain pub embellished with multifarious remnants of Hungary's communist era. Besides its terrific atmosphere and quirky decorations, the club has fantastic live music and cheap drinks as well.

Address: Kazinczy utca 14, Budapest 1075, Hungary

Contact number: +36 1 352 4198

Website: http://www.szimpla.hu/

Opening hours: 12 pm to 4 am daily

Manufactured surrealism with mind-blowing music

Like Szimpla Kert, Instant is a phenomenal rain pub that took the city by storm. A euphoric labyrinth with a dreamlike setting, Instant has over three bustling dance floors, six bars and 20 rooms. It has free entrance, and has twisting pathways with strange yet wonderful decorations. As for the music, the rain pub has heart-pounding break-beats as well as drum and bass tunes with a twist of jazz, indie and rock.

Address: VI., Nagymezo u. 38, Budapest 1065, Hungary

Contact number: +36 1 311 0704

Opening hours: 4 pm to 6 am

A spoonful of hard rock music

Is metal rock your cup of tea? Formerly known as Wigwan Rock Club, 202 Music Club is a vivid convert venue that has been a host to an endless number of notable international metal and rock acts, such as Iron Maiden, discharge, and a whole lot more.

Address: Budapest, Fehervari ut 202, 1116 Hungary

Contact number: +36 1 208 5569

Website: http://www.club202.hu/

Prices and schedule vary. Please refer to their website.

A trendy rooftop club with a zesty dance club

One of the hottest rooftop bars in the city, Corvinteto has reached the national limelight for its dynamic underground dance club, superb city skyline views, and affordable prices. As a matter of fact, it was once featured in The New York Times.

Address: Blaha Lujza ter 1-2, Budapest, Hungary

Contact number: +36 20 378 2988

http://corvinteto.hu/

Opening hours: 6 pm to 5 am Monday to Sunday

Hungarian jazz music at its best

Longing for cool and soothing jazz music? A jazz true lover's delight, the Budapest Jazz club is popular concert venue that showcases the newest talents and finest jazz musicians in the country. In addition, it has high-quality acoustics and cozy interior, making it a great place to hang out at night in Budapest. Aside from jazz musicians, the venue's stage has also been graced by well-known international and local bands performing a variety of genres, including Bossa Nova, classical music and salsa.

Address: Hollan Erno utca 7, Budapest 1136, Hungary

Contact number: +36 70 413 9837

Website: http://www.bjc.hu/

Opening hours: 6 pm to 4 am from Monday to Saturday. Closed on Sundays

A melting pot of modern Hungarian artists

Fogashaz is an ecstatic fusion of a ruin pub and cultural center, welcoming musicians, theatre groups and contemporary artists. A variety of late night programs are available throughout the week, such as theater performances and film screenings. A great venue to mingle with the friendly locals, the place has a large atmospheric courtyard with bouncy music from local DJs.

Address: Akacfa utca 51, Budapest 1073, Hungary

Contact number: +36 70 324 5281

Website: http://www.fogashaz.hu/

Opening hours: 10 am to 4 am from Monday to Saturday. 4 pm to 4 am on Sundays

5 ARTSY RELAXATION & A LAVISH SHOPPING SPREE

Revitalize your senses, cure your nasty hangover, and give your jaded limbs a much-needed rest with a visit to any of the numerous relaxing thermal baths or spa centers in Budapest. Famous for public houses and thermal waters, Hungary's capital city is indeed a nest to some of the best spa complexes in Europe. In fact, this European turf is often called the city of healing waters, due to a bathing culture that dates back to ancient Roman times, and thermal waters bubbling from the deeper regions.

As soon as you're done pampering yourself, treat yourself by shopping at the many boutiques of this beautiful city. Then, cap off your trip in ecstasy by relaxing in one of the city's lush and scenic parks.

The best places to indulge in a thermal bath in Budapest

Gellert Baths

Gellert Baths in Budapest. Photo credit: <u>Joe Mabel</u> via Flickrr

When it comes to aesthetic appeal, very few bathhouses in the entire world can rival the Gellert Baths in Budapest. Designed in a mesmerizing art nouveau style, this bathhouse mixes two of the best features of the city, remarkable architecture and therapeutic waters. From the rooms and pools to the entrance, it is practically surrounded with stunning Art deco stained glass windows, wall mosaics and sculptures. Even if you are not planning on getting wet, a visit to the Gellert Baths is something you should include in your travel itinerary. After all, it is the most photographed thermal bath in Europe.

As for its therapeutic properties, it has more than a dozen of pools, including three outdoor pools and a swimming pool. Furthermore, it offers foot and body massages, and other spa services. A helpful tip, try to get some sun, while allowing yourself to dry up at the outdoor patio. After this, you will definitely feel completely revitalized, and ready for more fun-filled activities.

> Address: Kelenhegyi ut 4, Budapest 1118, Hungary
>
> Contact number: + 36 1 466 6166
>
> Website: http://gellertspa.com/
>
> Opening hours: 6 am to 8 pm daily
>
> Recommended time of arrival: 8:30 to 9 am
>
> Duration: 1 to 2 hours
>
> Prices: 2,450 to 25,000 HUF

Szechenyi Bath

Szechenyi Bath. Photo credit: Graeme Churchard via Flickrr

Travelling with a bunch of friends? Located in City Park, the Szechenyi Bath is truly a terrific choice for those who want to enjoy a relaxing morning with their friends and family. Billing itself as Europe's largest medicinal bath, this public bath has a variety of pools to cater to everyone's preference. While the complex doesn't have slides, it has a pool specifically designed for kids.

Address: Budapest, Allatkerti korut 9-11, Hungary

Contact number: +36 1 363 3210

Website: http://www.szechenyifurdo.hu/

Opening hours: 6 am to 10 pm daily

Recommended time of arrival: 9:30 to 10 am

Duration: 1 to 2 hours

Prices: 500 to 4,500 HUF

Eat your lunch

Before you move on to the next activity, though, you need to break bread from a restaurant that would please your aesthetic taste. Even though this day isn't as active as the previous ones, you need some nourishment to help you sustain your activities. It's a day of artsy relaxation anyway, so nibble on all the guilty culinary pleasures that you want.

If you have decided to take a relaxing bath at Gellert Baths, you can eat your lunch at their small café, which serves a limited range of pancakes, sandwiches, wines and beers. Don't like sandwiches? Go to Hadik Coffee House, a legendary coffee with a pre-fixed lunch menu, and a decent selection of soups and appetizers.

Budapest, Bartok Belau t 36, 1111, Hungary

+36 1 279 0290

9 am to 11 pm Monday to Sunday

Recommended time of arrival: 11:30 am to 12 pm

Duration: 30 minutes to 1 hour

What about restaurants near Szechenyi Bath? Located on Adrassy Avenue, the Kogart Museum Restaurant is a lovely atmospheric restaurant that serves tasty Hungarian staples and healthy vegetarian dishes.

Addrassy ut 112, Budapest 1062, Hungary

+36 1 354 3830

Opening hours: 10 am to 6 pm Monday to Friday

Recommended time of arrival: 11:30 am to 12 pm

Duration: 30 minutes to 1 hour

Shop till you drop

Looking for designer stores and chain boutiques like Lacoste, Hugo Boss, Nike and H&M? Then, make your way to Vaci Utca, the premier and most fashionable shopping street in Hungary. In spite of the commercial factor and sporadic tourist traps, walking is quite pleasant in this area of the city.

As a shopper in this lively shopping district, make sure to drop by the small stores, as they offer decent quality leather goods like belts and shoes at very affordable prices.

> Address: Budapest 1056, Hungary
>
> Recommended time of arrival: 12:30 to 1 pm
>
> Opening hours: Hours vary from shop to shop. But in general, shops are open during this time.
>
> Duration: 1 hour

Prefer to shop in a mall? Head straight to the WestEnd City Center, which is one of the largest shopping malls in all of Central Europe. A Mecca for shoppers and fashion lovers, WestEnd City Center is a mall that has everything you need, displaying more than 50 jewelry stores, 60 shoe stores, 180 shops, and 300 clothing brands.

Address: WestEnd Ingatlanhasznosito es Uzemelteto Kft., Budapest 1062, Hungary

Contact number: +36 1 374 6573

From Vaci Utca, you take a 30-minute walk to this gigantic mall. Looking for a faster way to reach it? Take bus 950A, 950, 914A or 914.

Opening hours: 8 am to 11 pm daily

Recommended time of arrival: 3 pm

Duration: 1 hour

A peaceful and breezy respite in the midst of a zingy city

A fitting way to end a festive 3-day holiday in Hungary's capital is to relax and unwind at Margit Sziget, or also called Margaret Island. Set amidst the River Danube, Margaret Island is a laid-back sanctuary where you can enjoy outdoor activities, including biking, swimming and jogging. Also, it's a great place to take a picnic while enjoying its lush scenery.

What are the other things to do on this island? It

has a load of attractions, including an open-air theatre, water park, swimming pools, water tower, musical fountain, small zoo, medieval ruins and romantic walkways. The island is speckled with gorgeous old trees, flower gardens and large green areas.

Address: Margitsziget, Budapest 1138, Hungary

Opening hours: The park is open 24/7, but most shops and attractions on the island follow a schedule.

Recommended time of arrival: 5 pm

Duration: 1 to 2 hours

Getting there: Hop aboard tram 6 or 4, and make sure to get off at the Margit hud Budai hidfo stop. From Nyugati ter, you may also take bus 234 or 26. Keep in mind that driving is prohibited on the island.

6 THE BEST PLACES TO DINE IN HUNGARY'S FOOD CAPITAL

Budapest dining. Photo credit: <u>Liz Henry</u> via Flickrr

Finding a filling and yummy meal in this cosmopolitan destination won't be a problem for any foodie or tourist. From Michelin-star restaurants to small cafes and eateries, the city is oozing with dining centers that serve palatable

Hungarian dishes. Apart from Hungarian meals, you can sample every major international cuisine in this destination as well. Not to mention, it has a few exotic treats that would thrill gastronomers with an adventurous palate, such as the Great Market's horse meat.

Cheap eats

Kisharang Restaurant

Awarded with a certificate of excellence in 2014 by Tripadvisor, Kisharang Restaurant is a small, cozy and unpretentious restaurant with affordable rates, exemplary service and appetizing Hungarian mouthful goodies. Giving you a real taste of Budapest, this restaurant allows you savor a variety of authentic Hungarian food and signature dishes, such as Hortobagy pancakes, and goulash.

    1051 Oktober 6. U. 17, Budapest 1051, Hungary

    +36 1 269 3861

W35 Restaurant

Located right at the heart of Budapest, W35 Restaurant is a classic American street food joint that serves the juiciest and best tasting burgers in town. Aside from their mouthwatering burgers and other American staples, W35 also serves Mexican specialties, including burrito and quesadilla.

Wessenlenyi utca 35, Budapest 1077, Hungary

+36 1 796 5370

Mamo Gelato Restaurant

Craving for something sweet? Indulge in a nectarous scoop of genuine Italian gelato with a visit to the Mamo Gelato Restaurant. For a small place, the restaurant amazingly has a dozen of gelato varieties and extensive range of flavors.

Raday utca 24, Budapest, Hungary

+36 70 420 4259

Mid-range options

Hungarikum Bisztro Restaurant

With its attentive service and remarkable gastronomic pleasures, it is wonder the Hungarikum Bisztro Restaurant gets a ton of rave reviews from foodies and culinary experts. Often publicized as the premier Hungarian restaurant in Budapest, Hungarikum Bisztro Restaurant also has a dazzling collection of wines, nice live music, and a romantic ambiance.

A must try in this restaurant is the flavorful goulash soup with tender beef. Other delightful dishes offered in this restaurant include chicken-filled crepes with paprika sauce, crispy duck legs, and pork loin with tasty friend potatoes.

Steindl Imre utca 13, Budapest 1051, Hungary

+36 30 661 6244

Curry House Restaurant

Are you in the mood for something unique, healthy and spicy? Delight your taste buds with a true taste of India at the Curry House, the ultimate Indian restaurant in the city. Here, you get to feast upon the best lamb curries and vegetarian dishes in this food capital.

Horanszky utca 1, 1085 Budapest, Hungary

+36 1 264 0297

Taverna Dionysos Restaurant

The Taverna Dionysos Restaurant is a rare gem in the city's rich culinary scene. One of the very few Greek restaurants in the city, Taverna Dionysos Restaurant has a pleasant Mediterranean feel, and attentive service. More importantly, it has a diverse selection of sumptuous Greek food.

Belgrad Rakpart 16, Belvaros-Lipotvaros, Budapest 1056, Hungary

+36 1 318 1222

Deluxe Restaurants

Onyx

Onyx is a Michelin-starred restaurant that has added a new twist to the most beloved traditional dishes in the country. Modernizing the country's cuisine, this upscale restaurant delights its guests with its highly acclaimed "Hungarian Evolution", a piquant six-course menu. Furthermore, the restaurant has a beautiful atmosphere coupled with first-class service.

Vorosmarty Square 7 to 8, Budapest 1051,

Hungary

+36 30 508 0622

Paris Budapest Bar and Restaurant

A harmonious mixture of Hungarian and French cuisines, the Paris Budapest Bar and Restaurant is an exclusive restaurant with amazing views, mouthwatering French and Hungarian specialties as well as fabulous cocktails. Plus, it has a galore of fresh and appetizing seafood, including shark, sea razor, octopus, crabs, shrimps, oysters and fish.

Szechenyi Istvan ter 2, Sofitel Budapest Chain Bridge, Budapest, Hungary

+36 30 302 7885

Comme Chez Soi Restaurant

Do you love pastas and other Italian gastronomic treats? As far as Italian cuisine is concerned, Comme Chez Soi Restaurant is absolutely your best bet during your trip to this cosmopolitan hub. Not only does it have an authentic character and nostalgic ambiance, but it also has fast, attentive and efficient service. As for the food, the restaurant will delight you with large servings of your favorite Italian staples. Plus, the restaurant serves complementary Hungarian schnapps and homemade lemon chemo.

1051 Budapest, Aranykez u2, Budapest, Hungary

+36 1 318 3943

7 WHERE TO ENJOY A GOOD NIGHT'S SLEEP IN BUDAPEST

Hôtel Palazzo Zichy, Budapest. Photo credit: <u>Jean-François Gornet</u> via Flickrr

Are you on the lookout for a great place to stay in Budapest? Whether you are self-indulgent or a budget-conscious backpacker, Hungary's capital certainly has an accommodation that fits like a glove to your fiscal estimate and zest. From the five-star properties and epicurean guesthouses of Buda Hills to the converted flats and hostels of its downtown area, the city of Budapest offers a wide range of accommodations to its trippers.

Budget-friendly accommodations

Aboriginal Hostel

Do you prefer to stay in a hostel, and have a friendly chat with other backpackers? Functioning like a convivial shared apartment, this hotel is a place in which travelers meet, and get some helpful extras for their travel needs. Not only does it have a welcoming staff, but it also has an easygoing vibe, and a shared room where you can share and exchange your experiences with your fellow junketers. Plus, it has loads of treats, such as a cable television, and a home theatre with heaps of music collections and movies.

> Brody Sandor utca 46, First floor number 2, Budapest 1088, Hungary
>
> +36 30 405 8398

Gold Hotel Premium

With a relaxing feel and excellent location, the Gold Hotel Premium definitely makes a viable option, when choosing a budget-friendly accommodation in this cosmopolitan. A charming eco-friendly enclave, this hotel has spacious and immaculately clean rooms with a fast and reliable free WiFi.

14 Hegyalija Way, Budapest 1016, Hungary

http://www.goldhotel.hu/

Agape Guesthouse

Looking for a centrally-located and cushy place that doesn't cost a fortune? Located in the midst of Hungary's bustling capital, the Agape Guesthouse is a great base for sightseers who want to be mesmerized by the beautiful heritage sites of the city. As for its accommodations, it has private rooms with clean bathrooms, and a ton of amenities. Also, it has a few appealing rooms with balconies that provide striking cityscape views.

Budapest, Akacfa utca 12, 1072 Hungary

+36 1 317 4833

Mid-range enclaves

Casati Budapest Hotel

Formerly known as Hotel Pest, the Casati Budapest Hotel is within walking distance to everything worth visiting and seeing in this city. Besides its ideal location, it is fairly clean, and has a very tasteful décor as well. To add more pleasure to your stay in this hotel, Casati Budapest Hotel also has a relaxing cellar with a massage, fitness and sauna room.

Paulay Ede u. 31, Budapest 1051m Hungary

+36 1 343 1198

Three Corners Hotel Art

Set in the serene side street of Budapest's downtown area, the Three Corners Hotel Art is a stylish budget hotel with an excellent location. As a guest in this hotel, you get easy access to the Danube embankment as well as a handful of restaurants, bars and attractions. Housed in a historic building, this hotel is also fully air-conditioned, and has a number of niceties, including a sauna, fitness room, café, bar and restaurant.

Kirali Pal Utca 12, Budapest, Hungary

+36 1 266 2166

B018 Hotel Superior

One of top-rated hotels in the city, B018 Hotel Superior has everything you need for a relaxing stay in this destination. Known for its high standards in courtesy, cleanliness and comfort, B018 Hotel Superior is indeed a quality hotel with spacious rooms, helpful staff, amazing amenities, and a contemporary design.

Vajdahunyad utca 18, district VIII, Budapest, Hungary

+36 1 469 3526

Deluxe accommodations

Four Seasons Hotel Gresham Palace

Touted as the ultimate luxury hotel in Budapest, the Four Seasons Hotel Gresham Palace delights its guests with its refined service and elegant ambiance. As a guest in this hotel, you get to relax under a large and loose-fitting room with fabulous bathroom, and a collection of pleasantries. Likewise, it is within walking distance from some of Budapest's most celebrated points of interests.

> Szechenyi Istvan ter 5-6, Budapest 1051, Hungary

> +36 1 268 6000

Hotel Palazzo Zichy

Hotel Palazzo Zichy is, without a doubt, the most romantic and surreal luxury hotel in the city. Famed for its nostalgic charm, the hotel offers a cluster of well-equipped, clean and comfortable rooms with a slew of facilities and amenities.

> Budapest, Lorinc pap ter 2, 1088 Hungary

> +36 1 235 4000

CONCLUSION

Budapest is a starry-eyed Hungarian dream full of life and mind-blowing surprises. Known as one of the most delightful cities in Europe, this beautiful city has the grandeur and grace of the continent's two most glamorized destinations, Vienna and Paris.

Even still, it has the cultural buzz and dynamic vibe of an age-old Eastern Bloc boom town that emerges from its fierce past.

Meshing natural wonders, grassy parks and old architectures with modern amazements, Budapest is an enchanting destination that you surely want to see and visit more than once in your life.

From sightseeing to shopping, there are a lot of things you can do and enjoy in Budapest in 72 hours or less. Whether you are fond of art, culture, partying, history or contemporary engineering spectacles, a three-day trip to this city gives you a plethora of joyous memories that you'll cherish for years to come. But, if you want to extend your stay, and discover more of the city, go ahead, and enjoy the rest Budapest has to offer. Bucsu!

MORE FROM THIS AUTHOR

Below you'll find some of our other books that are popular on Amazon and Kindle as well. Alternatively, you can visit our author page on Amazon to see other work done by us.

3 Day Guide to Berlin: A 72-hour definitive guide on what to see, eat and enjoy in Berlin, Germany

3 Day Guide to Vienna: A 72-hour definitive guide on what to see, eat and enjoy in Vienna Austria

3 Day Guide to Santorini: A 72-hour definitive guide on what to see, eat and enjoy in Santorini Greece

3 Day Guide to Provence: A 72-hour definitive guide on what to see, eat and enjoy in Provence, France

3 Day Guide to Istanbul: A 72-hour definitive guide on what to see, eat and enjoy in Istanbul, Turkey

3 Day Guide to Budapest: A 72-hour Definitive Guide on What to See, Eat and Enjoy in Budapest, Hungary

Printed in Great Britain
by Amazon.co.uk, Ltd.,
Marston Gate.